Piecing It Together:

Feminism and Nonviolence

Feminism and Nonviolence
Study Group

Many thanks to all those who have helped with publication of this pamphlet by loans or donations and to housemates and co-workers for their patience while we have been writing it. Thanks too to photographers for the use of their work, to City Limits (London) for help with picture research, and to Jennifer Tiffany for her hard work on our behalf in North America.

Published by The Feminism and Nonviolence Study Group
2 College Close, Buckleigh, Westward Ho, Devon EX39 1BL,
England in co-operation with the War Resisters' International
55 Dawes Street, London SE17 1EL, England.

Information about North American trade distribution and
individual mail order from our American agent:
Jennifer Tiffany, 525 South Danby Road, Spencer, NY 14883, USA

Mail order and inquiries about foreign distribution outside North
America from The Feminism and Nonviolence Study Group.

This book is also available on tape — inquiries as above.

Typeset in 10pt Century and printed by Calvert's Press Ltd (TU),
55 Mount Pleasant, London WC1, England (Tel: 01-278 7177).

CONTENTS

Introduction

It has become clear to us that resistance to war and to the use of nuclear weapons is impossible without resistance to sexism, to racism, to imperialism and to violence as an everyday pervasive reality. There is a profound relationship between the fact that individual women are commonly attacked and beaten up and that a nuclear war threatens the entire world.

We've written this pamphlet in the belief that many basic ideas are held in common by feminists and by those advocating non-violence. We also feel that the current peace movement does not take adequate account of the ideas and experiences of feminism. For example, women's actions are still perceived as divisive by many people. At the same time, certain women's actions for peace can tend to perpetuate our subordination by portraying women as natural peacemakers and not as powerful activists for change. This works against our liberation rather than for it.

Both feminism and nonviolence express the belief that the world we know is not as it should be and this can be changed. They are, to a large extent, responses to those immensely powerful forces which would destroy us. In order to appreciate the radical challenge and depths of feminism and nonviolence we have to look at exactly what they are in response to.

The experience of the Falklands War provided us with some very concrete examples. In the patriotic euphoria, the moral and political issues were all swept under the carpet. Few asked questions about the cost in human life, or the diplomatic errors that resulted in sending out young men to fight, or the possibilities of finding other means to settle the islands' future. Few enquired about who was supplying the arms and making the money — and those who did were generally ignored or called 'traitors'.

The rows over the role of the media highlighted the saying that the first casualty of war is truth. It was the media, too, which gave us a very good idea of the expected role of women in war-time. The faces of two grieving women — one Argentinian, one British — dominated the front page of *The Times* one day in May 1982: both had lost sons or husbands in the war, and the photos caused a storm of protest. By showing the human consequences of war to be the same for women on both 'sides', the media were apparently 'not supporting Britain'. The government wanted propaganda, not truth. The hastily coined word 'Argies' symbolised, too, the instant de-humanising process directed against every Argentinian.

In the Falklands War, as in all other situations where the State uses violence, a mechanism comes into play which renders the brutality both acceptable and justifiable. Whether humans or animals are the victims, there is a distancing of the observer from those on whom the pain is inflicted. But violence *against* the State is instantly portrayed as both unacceptable and illegitimate, and those people who struggle against violent injustice, as in Poland, South Africa or Northern Ireland, are labelled 'terrorists'. Might is right, and the weak are always wrong, especially if they fight back.

One reason for this is that many people do not recognise any forms of violence other than physical violence, whereas for us violence includes conditions which themselves kill. Poverty, hunger and racism degrade individuals and inflict suffering. Some massacres are considered newsworthy, but we also know that thousands die daily from starvation, neglect, lack of clean water or medical supplies. Yet when physical violence erupts in response to the built-in violence that perpetuates these conditions, the participants are depicted as less than human and without any motivation for their violence. Those who expose the roots of inequality have to be outlawed, punished and silenced.

This built-in violence has become so invisible that personal experiences of physical violence are often seen as isolated incidents. They are not; they are part of the spectrum of violence that runs through our culture. When a woman is battered or raped, she is often treated not as the victim but the wrong-doer by police and courts. The violence of the National Front is not challenged by a society run by whites, while racism is enshrined in the laws of the country. Personal violence reflects the systematic violence of our society. The organised violence inflicted on people in the context of a war is an extension of that inflicted on one person by another, and of the violence of a system which pretends that everyone is equal whilst discriminating openly, through its schools, media, police and legal system.

In a society which visibly rewards aggression and successful violence, both feminism and nonviolence demand a certain type of human behaviour and present challenges to authority. It does not come easily to be nonviolent, and it is harder still to see nonviolence as an assertive, imaginative form of resistance. Many people decry and dismiss the idea of it as an alternative to violent resistance, even when the latter is obviously failing to achieve its aims. Unlike traditional armed struggle, nonviolence gives everyone a chance to be involved on an equal basis, not just the young, fit and (generally) male. In situations where social change is demanded, it gives the participants greater control, and thus more power.

This country does not have a very strong tradition of conscious nonviolence, and many here know of it only vaguely as a method

JONATHAN PRICE

The traditional role of women in time of war is to watch and wait — while the men march away.

used by a few exceptional men, such as Gandhi in India and Martin Luther King in the USA. In fact, it has been widely used with success by many people, and though most of the well-known theoreticians are men, many women have initiated nonviolent direct action for change. For example, it was Mrs Gandhi who actually gave Mahatma Gandhi the idea for the campaign of resistance which led to independence for India. It was Rosa Parkes whose refusal to give up her seat on the bus which sparked off the Black civil rights movement in the USA. While many women, such as Ethel Mannin, Dorothy Day, Coretta King, Peggy Smith, Dolores Huerta and countless others, have made enormous contributions as women to nonviolent struggles, they are not so well known as the men. Nothing new in that!

However, this is not a guide to 'famous women' or 'women who ought to be more famous', but rather a statement of those principles which have moved us in this group to action ourselves. Part of our political outlook is not to mimic the male superstar system but to credit everyone associated in the effort to create effective change. The woman or man who stays at home to look after the children participates as crucially as the person who climbs the fence or goes to jail. We believe that honesty, determination, working together,

7

recognising the links between different struggles and using our imaginations *can* prevail — even in the face of the powers that deny us as people and risk destroying our future and that of the earth.

In the pamphlet, we begin by examining the most blatant and visibly destructive form of violence: war. War epitomises the violence in our society today, reflecting the institutions which are themselves the products òf certain basic principles and assumptions. From war, therefore, we move to a brief look at patriarchy, capitalism 'and the State, together with the institutions which uphold them, such as the law, the media and the welfare state. The second section outlines our theoretical basis for bringing about change, using feminism and nonviolence as cornerstones. Women have been on the receiving end of all kinds of violence for centuries, and the third section looks at how some feminists today respond to it. We also look at the most recent development: large numbers of women active *as women* in the peace movement. We close, appropriately, with our vision of a future society based on the changes we are working to bring about.

Women have moved into the front line of the struggle for peace. Blockade of Greenham Common airbase, March 1982.

CHAPTER 1

The World We Live In

Women and War

War is the most extreme form of organised violence. Nonviolent activists traditionally explain why they oppose war. But as nonviolent feminists we must go further and explain how sexual divisions in society operate to support and perpetuate wars.

All the dictionary definitions of war as a 'quarrel between nations conducted by force' or a 'contest between armed forces' — let alone the militarist's crack that it is 'the continuation of policy by other means' — give us no real picture of what it means when large numbers of people kill and are killed. Governments may decide to go to war for a number of reasons, either economic or to reinforce some basic element of the system which we define as patriarchal later in this chapter. But how are ordinary people persuaded to participate in a process which leads, all too frequently in the modern world, to genocide — that is the murder of people for no other reason than that they 'belong' to a particular racial, national or political grouping?

There are two principle ways in which people are led to support and participate in wars: by coercion and by persuasion. Coercion exists or is created in such forms as conscription, both into the armed forces and the industry needed to sustain them; or as military discipline whereby those who try to run away from shooting other people are shot; or by a variety of laws or practices which allow civilians, their goods or services to be 'commandeered' for the war effort. But it is by ideological means, both the direct propaganda of the State and the more insidious, indirect propaganda of the media, that people are persuaded to believe in any given war as 'just'.

In times of crisis, particularly when war is threatened, it becomes crucial for there to be an appearance of national harmony and cohesion, whilst at the same time the individual's sense of impotence is subtly increased to prevent any domestic opposition. People are told that they are fighting *for* some concept beyond their own immediate safety, though this too is constantly emphasised. Thus in western countries we are told we are fighting for 'freedom and democracy', though parliamentary democracy is the first institution to go in time of all-out war and more than one village in

Vietnam was razed to the ground to keep it 'free'. In the Second World War we were 'fighting fascism', but those who had gone to fight fascism in Spain in the preceding three years were condemned as 'premature' anti-fascists because the British government did not want to support Republican Spain.

A powerful and common mechanism of control, used frequently by the rulers of society, is a steady and systematic denial of basic human qualities. People gradually become unfeeling, a false notion of honour is developed and men especially learn to relate to the world from a distance. The media plays its part in this: people have become accustomed to fighting, pain and death daily on their television screens and in their newspapers; it becomes possible to manipulate reactions and responses. We are prepared for the advent of war by continual images of violence and suffering the world over, presented as inevitable in the 'real ' world.

It becomes hard to differentiate between real pictures of death and destruction and fictitious ones, when the news is generally sandwiched between programmes liberally offering shooting and sexual violence. In this way it is not difficult for war reporting to be censored so that we are only allowed to see the reality of death and destruction when it is deemed appropriate. We can thus be encouraged to identify with those suffering when it is politically expedient — witness the public declarations of distress provoked by the plight of the security forces in Ireland or the victims of the Ballykelly bombing, or the British men killed in the Falklands. When has there been any recognition of the suffering felt by IRA men who have been shot or the people who love them or the Argentinians who lost their lives?

Central to the success of this alienation, and to the stability of the status quo, is the notion that women's and men's roles in life are quite distinct, and that women are inferior. As women, we are taught that we are second class citizens and have no effective jurisdiction over the world, no right to interfere or protest at its destruction — our place is in the home. Consequently most of us end up pouring our energies into the care and maintenance of others. In peace, it is men who are meant to go out to work, while women stay at home to fulfil their 'natural' function as mothers.

Yet in a war the ideology which promotes and perpetuates this role is swiftly reversed. Women are encouraged to put their children in day-care, ordered to take up their place in the munitions factories and 'do their bit for the duration'. As soon as the crisis has passed and peace is apparently secured again, the original and long-term ideology reasserts itself: yesterday's efficient factory worker must transform overnight into an unwaged housewife so that the demobbed soldier can have 'his' job back. So, though women have often found independence during war-time, both economic and emotional,

10

this is only a small hiccup in the ideology: we are now supposed to get on preparing our children to be sucked into the same dehumanising cycle.

Raising children is one of the best examples of how we women have largely adapted ourselves to the demands of the traditional value system, in the process of which our basically fine motives are transformed to make us servants of the status quo. Rearing a child is an enormous task, the female energy invested in her or him is continuous — developing the child's ability to walk and talk, make friends, learn to deal with upsets, take all the very slow steps to independence. Because of the way society is organised, it often becomes a non-stop, 24 hours a day, seven days a week responsibility. The child or children are totally absorbing, taking precedence over most other things.

This nurturing role is something we are conditioned to accept, rather than choosing freely for ourselves. Yet, because the rewards can be enormous, many women go ahead with having children, even recognising the dangers that await them, growing up in this society, prominent among which is the likely toll of war. When a soldier or civilian is killed, twenty years or more of the fruits of one woman's labour is destroyed. The woman will never be able to enjoy seeing her children achieve their full potential. This will be not by accident, but wilfully, because someone, somewhere, who could not appreciate the value of human life, issued an order.

In many ways women are still close to the essence of human life. Women's work and traditional role is bound up intrinsically with it. Whether we have had children or not, our upbringing will probably have revolved around our future motherhood. We are taught how to communicate with others, how to understand another person's needs, and how to fulfil them — and we have undoubtedly benefited from this. But it's gone too far, too many of us have been imbued with a compulsion to sacrifice ourselves to serve others.

Men, too, have suffered (though not been oppressed by) sexism. Society has kept them at arm's length from the magic of human life and this separation has had very dire consequences. It has meant most men are more likely to see human beings as expendable, and can be conned into feeling a sense of glory in dying for their loved ones, people or country. This is a denial of the worth of human life, and confuses the issue of when it can be worthwhile to lay down one's life for a cause. Many people label conscientious objectors as cowards, with little conception of the courage and human and political insight they need to resist the wartime propaganda machine and its attendant social values.

Men are taught a value system where basic common sense is contradicted again and again. Even laudable values get twisted to serve the god of financial gain. Love of one's country turns into

Treating women as sex objects contributes to the 'distancing' from other people and is used in training soldiers to kill. Chattenden Barracks, Kent, were opened in 1966 with pin-up boards as an official fixture.

aggression towards foreigners, and, whilst it is possible to die honourably for a cause, deaths in conventional war have much more to do with preserving territory for the ruling class than with honour. Men are encouraged to be confident, but also to be insensitive to other people's needs, to act fearlessly, but not to show they are scared. They learn the supposed virtue of scientific detachment, then cannot relate their findings to human need and ecological balance. Short cuts to save money lead to grave environmental pollution and possible nuclear meltdowns.

In films, and in real life, we see the heroes being sent off to fight, while their wives and sweethearts bravely let them go, dabbing their eyes, but not actually intervening in the process. Next we are shown the joyful hugs on their return or the proud sorrow of those whose husbands or boyfriends, sons, fathers or brothers have died for their country. But what are we women really doing whilst 'keeping the home fires burning? Certainly not spending our time looking wistfully out to sea, but concentrating on the increased work of keeping a home, family and, by extension, a whole country's economy going. In time of war, women suddenly become single parents, valuable workers needed to do 'men's jobs' and overtime, and morale boosters for 'our boys over there'. Money channelled into the war, and military spending generally, mean that women are expected to increase their capacity to make do with less food, fuel and space to live, while many social services and other facilities which don't contribute directly to the war effort are withdrawn.

That is what *we* do. But what about the women on the 'other side'? They are making do as much as we are. But how do 'our boys' view them? With contempt, as part of the booty of war. Individual soldiers are encouraged to celebrate the possession of a territory by the possession of an 'enemy' woman. The incidence of rape in war, and later denial of it, has been minutely documented by Susan Brownmiller, in her book *Against Our Will*, and its universal occurrence suggests that women will always be war victims.

We are told that this is an 'unfortunate' spin-off of the soldiers' healthy lust for victory, but we see it rather as the brutalising effect that war experience has on its perpetrators and an extension of everyday patriarchal attitudes. The effect of continually witnessing atrocity is to dehumanise everyone in the eye of the observer, who becomes hardened to those weaker than himself.

It's not unusual, either, for large numbers of women to be subjected to mass rape as retaliation for a military action by the enemy. From the male aggressors' point of view, although it is the women who suffer it is the men who are being attacked, via 'their property' (women). We begin to wonder whose idea it was that we needed protection. Is it us who are being protected or men's sense of property? According to social values, women need a man to protect us from other men; and we need an army to protect us from invading armies. But in a context where the invasion of women's bodies is an accepted consequence of war, this protection is worth very little. Indeed, who will protect us from our protectors?

Women are traditionally seen as the 'passive' victims of war, but the last ten years have also seen a dramatic increase in the recruitment of women in Western armed forces — often in the name of 'equality'. We fundamentally disagree with the idea that women's liberation has been furthered by an increased female contribution to the armies of the world. Liberation can never occur within an institution of repression and destruction. Inherent in the meaning of feminism is liberation for all. There is no doubt that some individual women have benefited from their connection with the armed forces but womankind and our natural allies, all other oppressed people, do not benefit from the existence of a force used to uphold a society which does not serve our interest.

Even in its own terms, the integration of women into the army as a route to emancipation is a failure. For example, the Israeli army, well known for its women soldiers, has 'failed to challenge traditional and very basic sexist ideologies', according to Nira Yuval-Davis in *Loaded Questions*. Equal opportunity in the army is a myth. Apart from the few token women in non-traditional jobs, the vast majority of women in the army still reflect the sexual division of labour in civilian life. The women service the men, who do the 'real work' at the front or operating the sophisticated technology controlling modern weapons. Women service the army by being nurses, clerical workers and prostitutes.

Of course, there have always been war-mongering women, some of them even get to be heads of State, many of them have had children. Being mothers proves they are 'real women' and they now have a chance to graduate as a person or, more accurately, as a substitute man. To take that step out of the home and into public life is still a big move for a woman and, like most immigrants unsure of their welcome, they are likely to obey the dominant rules of the receiving culture. To succeed in the world they must accept its values.

But many women will no longer accept that the only alternatives for our future lie with one or other version of the existing system. We are appalled at the complacency of our society towards present and future atrocity, and motivated to take action. We feel an instinctive horror, and as feminists our drive to do something about it is substantiated by our deep desire for liberation for ourselves and all other oppressed people. We see that women playing a leading role in changing the world is a basic ingredient for peace. We have to be prepared to take on this role if we say we don't like the way the world is now. And we *don't* like the way it is now.

14

Going to the Roots

When we are trying to rid the world of things as oppressive as nuclear weapons or poverty, sexism or racism, it can help to look at their structural underpinning — the system of patriarchy, with capitalism and the State as basic and linked aspects of that system. People may argue about which came first (and sometimes therefore which should be confronted first) but we are more concerned to understand their interconnectedness and how they affect our society now. We also see that it is important to struggle against all three and the various ways in which they show themselves. Individuals (including those in this group!) may put more energy into changing one aspect than another, but tackling only one, for instance getting the British State to disarm without digging out the roots of men's oppression of women, would not make for very deep or lasting change.

Patriarchy

We see patriarchy as a system of male domination, prevalent in both capitalist and socialist countries, which is oppressive to women and restrictive to men. It is a hierarchical system in which men have more 'value', more social and economic power, and under which women suffer both from oppressive structures and from individual men. It shows itself clearly in all areas of our lives, affecting politi-

ANDREW WIARD/REPORT

15

cal and economic structures, our work, our homes, our personal relationships. Put bluntly, men are at the centre of a patriarchal world — whether they want to be or not.

While other structures of domination exist — like that of nation over nation, economic class over class, race over race — the domination of women by men remains a constant feature within every other aspect of oppression. It is so basic to our world that it is seen by most men, and many women, as part of 'human nature' and therefore something which cannot be changed. No pattern of domination is necessarily part of 'human nature', whether it be individual acts of rape or total war. Norms of human behaviour *can* and *do* change over the centuries and these aspects can be changed too. But because the oppression of women is so deeply embedded in all societies and in our psyches and because it is accepted as natural, it can remain virtually invisible, even to those who are working to change other sorts of injustice.

Capitalism

A capitalist society is one where the social structure is based on the economic exploitation of one group by another. Capitalism involves a working process in which 'the means of production' (such as a factory and the machines in it) are owned by one group, the capitalist class, but the people who actually do the work, the workers, own neither the means of production nor the wealth they produce. Thus the buying and selling of labour is done in the same way as with any other sort of commodity: the owner and the worker enter into a contract of exchange in which the labour power of a worker is bought in return for a wage.

The contract is not an equal one, however, because the owners have the control and therefore more power. It is unequal, too, because the worker produces a surplus, which is translated into profits for the capitalist. Thus a wage never reflects the true value of the goods produced, as the price they are sold at includes a surplus which might get ploughed back into the firm or go straight into the owner's pocket. This profit then is essentially kept out of the hands of those who made it.

As a result of work by the trade unions and other labour movement organisations, the workers in advanced capitalist countries, like Britain, now have a larger share of the wealth they create, but they still do not own the factories, nor have the power to control what is produced. They might own their own homes and a range of consumer goods but this does not make them part of the capitalist class.

The capitalist State could not have arisen and flourished solely on the backs of the indigenous working class. Capitalists had to institute imperialism abroad, as well as racism at home, to attain their present position. For example, 19th century Lancashire cotton magnates relied on the suppression of the indigenous textile industry of India for their near-world monopoly, whilst ruthlessly exploiting British workers. Microchip technology relies heavily on the exploitation of millions of young women workers in South East Asia. Currently, multi-national corporations have developed to such an extent that they operate outside the control of any individual State, yet in some instances they completely dominate a national economy. Meanwhile, in those countries where people were brought in to boost the labour force in times of economic expansion, such workers are subject to both individual and institutionalised racism.

Because the aim of capitalism is the acquisition of wealth for a few people rather than fulfilling basic human needs, violence is experienced by the majority of the population at every stage of the production process, from the uranium miner in Namibia who contracts lung cancer, via the factory worker who loses a hand in a machine because proper safety precautions 'cost too much', to those kicked off the working process and made unemployed to suit the needs of exploitative economic policies.

An intrinsic part of an industrialised country's economy is its arms trade: not only is money made directly out of selling death-dealing merchandise, but that money is taken away from vital services like hospitals and schools, which would improve people's lives, particularly in the Third World where 62 per cent of arms are sold.

In 1979 the Indian government spent US$6 per head of the population on the military, but only US$2 a head on health.

17

The State

The State arose both as a result of the patriarchal urge to control and dominate and as a way of organising and perpetuating a particular set of economic and social relations, in Britain's case, capitalism. It is a specific way of organising society within a given (should we say stolen?) geographical territory. The organisation is intended both to protect physical boundaries from other States and to preserve the specific social, economic and political relations within those boundaries.

The State is not simply a single institution: it is a form of relations based on class exploitation. This is as true of supposedly social-ist States, such as the USSR, as for capitalist ones, though the nature of the class system is somewhat different. The way in which the State maintains these relationships is two-fold. Firstly, by the use, or threat, of organised violence (the military, the police and the sanctions of the law) and secondly by reinforcing social and economic relations through ideology, for example, the education system, the media and the Church.

Of course these social relations within the State, like economic relations, are also subject to change: in Britain, opposition outside and even within Parliament has produced some improvement, such as health and safety regulations at work or family allowances paid directly to women with children. In particular, the modern welfare state can be seen both as the result of working class struggle — for health, education and welfare benefits — and as a complex mechanism founded upon exploitative mechanisms such as sexism, and class oppression. It also reduces people's ability to control their lives, and increases dependency on the centralised State. At the same time, laws such as the Emergency Powers Acts make clear that real power within the State is not held in Parliament but in the hands of the Cabinet, the top levels of civil servants, the military and the police.

The continuum of violence emanating from patriarchal power pervades all our lives, from the nuclear family to the nuclear state. It is violence or the threat of violence, which helps to keep us power-less and which we are likely to meet as we start to struggle, whether it is an individual woman trying to change her relationship with a man or striking workers who meet police violence and arrest on the picket line.

One aspect of the State with which we are particularly con-cerned in this pamphlet is the armed forces. Armed forces exist os-tensibly to defend the nation state and all it purports to stand for, whether 'peace and socialism' or 'freedom and democracy', in short something we are told is 'ours'. But what is being defended is not 'ours' — land we do not own, a social system we do not control — but the interests of a powerful privileged minority. The final extension

The army can and does intervene in industrial disputes. Here a medical corps stands by to break a one-day strike by London ambulance drivers, June 1981.

of this lie is to tell us our 'freedom' will be preserved by nuclear holocaust.

The armed forces have another role, however, and that is to preserve the State from 'the enemy within'. Apart from within Northern Ireland it is uncommon to see the military on duty on the streets of a western country, yet an elaborate — and largely secret — system of emergency planning makes the intervention of the military possible, very fast and without resort to Parliament. So while most 'law and order' situations, like mass pickets, demonstrations or riots, are tackled by the police (themselves becoming increasingly militarised), the army stands only a pace back, ready when needed. Moreover, the fear of such violence can be enough to prevent many people from acting in the first place.

Underlying patriarchy, capitalism and the State is the most pervasive assumption of all: that some people are better than others and are therefore more important and valuable. This assumption expresses itself in the hierarchical structures which characterise our society at all levels. For example, on a building site, the man who writes the tender for a contract is considered of more value than the male manual worker who builds the houses, and is rewarded as such in terms of money and status. The building worker in his turn is considered more valuable and is more highly paid than the woman who runs the site canteen. Other forms of domination include those of adults over children, white over black, industrialised world over Third World and rich over poor.

Running parallel with these social divisions is the attitude which says that human beings are not a part of the diversity of life on earth, but a controlling force and somehow superior to the rest of the natural world. Other forms of life and the resources of the earth are viewed as exploitable by most contemporary cultures and especially the dominant ones. Rather than understanding the earth as an intricate life support system which is vulnerable and requires to be treated with care and respect, it is viewed as a gigantic toy to be played with until it has no further use and is broken. Only in reality the 'toy' will be irreparably damaged and our world could become a radioactive desert devoid of any life form at all.

Closely allied with this exploitative attitude is the notion of progress, a notion which presumes against much of the evidence, that life on earth in all its aspects is improving, and should be doing so. (This idea has been so basic to the thinking of Western culture for so long that even movements, like socialism, consciously attempting to break with established politics, are based on it.) This attitude encourges the belief that economic growth — in terms of more and more goods to be produced and consumed — can be infinite (those who now have no cars will have one, that those who have one will have two, and so on). Yet the evidence is that economic growth is not only failing, but is also being confined more and more to certain countries, such as the USA, and within those countries, to certain classes. Thus the price of this supposed universal growth is a deepening division in the world, with more and more people unemployed or starving.

To incorporate properly the notion of progress, society accepts that all technological developments are good and that any problems posed by them can always be solved. Take, for example, the ecological disasters that are caused throughout the world in pursuit of greater agricultural production. Synthetic fertilisers which diminish the productivity of the soil in the long term are being used to particular detriment in the Third World to produce crops which are often not even for home consumption. Not only are local farmers encouraged to abandon traditional fertilising methods in favour of buying imported manufactured goods they can barely afford, but there is a build-up in the soil of inorganic petro-chemicals whose deleterious effects the macho wizards of modern science have no way of eradicating. Thus initiatives which are presented as trying to alleviate world hunger are in fact yet another arrogant disruption of the ecological balance by the patriarchal industrialised world. The experts are terrified of being seen as so 'unmanly' as to change direction and admit that such activities were a mistake, or worse still, of people realising that lies had been told about the state of scientific competence or the real intentions of the advocates of such schemes. The cost could be the earth.

20

Structures of Oppression

For many peace activists, 'peace' means simply an absence of war; for nuclear disarmers it may mean specifically a world without nuclear weapons. But for us, since our basic definition of society is that it is both patriarchal and capitalist, peace means more than that: it means eradicating the causes of war and violence from our society.

We outlined above the organised violence of the military by which the patriarchal State keeps its power against the 'enemy' without and within. The ideology of patriarchy, capitalism and the State are also expressed through various forms of what many people in the peace movement call 'structural violence', that is institutions, such as the law, media or the welfare state , which perpetuate people's existing social and economic relations. The way ideology works is to use these institutions to convey the belief that everyone is united in thought and action in support of existing societal relations. Thus no habitual recourse to physical violence is required to maintain the status quo, which can be done in an apparently more civilised manner by the use of ideological controls.

Most sorts of ideological control function at two levels: they provide some clear and obvious advantages for the individual while at the same time regulating the individual's perceptions and actions. So, for example, newspapers and television serve a valuable function in giving us information about the world, but because the information is selected, biased and censored we are also subtly told what to think about it. In a society where supportive, social relations are hard to develop, the family fulfils a positive function as well as being the basic unit through which patriarchal ways are reproduced. The provisions of the welfare state, such as unemployment benefit or the National Health Service provide an essential safety net for people's survival under capitalism; yet at the same time they also perpetuate division and oppression based on class, gender and race. Similar things could be said of education, or religion or the law.

As feminists, we see the family as one of the most important places where the suppression of women, the nourishment of capitalism and the perpetuation of patriarchal values takes place. While men, and even women, gain important benefits such as some economic and emotional security from the family, its *ideological* function is to keep women in subjection, mould children into sex roles and condition people into believing that patriarchal authority is 'normal'. Thus the nuclear family reinforces men's power: women, once married, become socially — and in some respects legally — the possessions of men as well as usually being economically dependent on them. This form of structural violence also erupts frequently into physical violence:

21

JEREMY NICHOLL

Fascism is an expression both of authoritarianism and the patriarchy. In one sense the machismo it encourages — tough, rigid and brutal — is only an extension of normal masculine conditioning within the family.

She was punched in the side of her face, dragged screaming to the ground by her hair and pulled along the street, while passers-by and four men in a nearby garage stood and watched because they thought the man was her husband. *(Worcester Evening News)*

The family also serves to reinforce heterosexuality as an institution rather than as a free expression of sexual choice; lesbians and gay men struggle for freedom, whilst heterosexuality continues as the norm from which anything else is a deviation. The 'ordinary family' is the first and most important place where sex roles are learned and enforced: boys are conditioned to be tough, aggressive, adventurous and to concentrate on their intellect whilst repressing their feelings, while girls are taught to be caring, gentle, submissive, manipulative and to concentrate on feelings — their own and other people's. Not only are human attributes divided and stuck like labels onto the two sexes, but the 'feminine' attributes are constantly belittled. Lip-service is paid to their value but they are not acknowledged, while the 'masculine' ones are played up as both better and the human 'norm', and are duly rewarded. The result of sexism is not only the systematic oppression of women by men, it also severely inhibits the possibility of men developing their sensitive characteristics.

Women's place in a patriarchal society, existing primarily as wives and mothers and for the use of men, is reinforced not only in the family but by institutions of the welfare state such as the Department of Health and Social Security. For just as an individual man may feel he owns his wife, to the extent of 'having the right' to have sex or take out his aggressions on her, so unemployment and social security laws and practice underline the idea that women who live with men do not exist in their own right. For example, the cohabitation rule, whereby a woman is deemed to be supported by any man she may have a close relationship with and therefore not able to claim benefits is only one example of this, married women's inability to claim Supplementary Benefit in their own right another.

Racism too is perpetuated through the institutions of structural violence and reflects their sexist dimension. Dozens of deportation cases have been fought in recent years by black women who, through no fault of their own, have left or been left by husbands, only to find that this means they can no longer claim their full welfare benefits as long as their status and future in Britain remains under threat. In the eyes of the legislators, black women have no independent right to exist at all.

The law likewise regards a woman's life as less valuable than a man's. In June 1981 Gordon Asher was given a six months suspended sentence for strangling his 'unfaithful' wife. At the end of

JONATHAN PRICE

Advertising helps create pressures on women — how we should look, dress and behave — which few can conform to and under which some of us crack.

1980 the Maw sisters were sentenced to three years imprisonment for killing their extremely violent father in self-defence, whilst only three days before in the same court in Leeds Douglas Coles was given two years' probation for killing his wife.

All these forms of structural violence, and numerous others, are how the patriarchal State maintains exploitative relationships between groups of people within society. As well as being damaging in collective terms, structural violence injures the well-being and self-esteem of the individual. For example, girls are subtly encouraged to fail at school — in certain subjects, at least — in order to fulfil their allotted role of being less clever than men. Women's right to self-determination and an independent existence is denied, whilst we are bombarded with messages about how we should look and behave which, try as we may, most of us fail to conform to. We internalise our oppression, finding ways of blaming ourselves for being too loud, too clever, too fat. Under the pressure created by these contradictions many of us break down and, raging and grieving for our stolen lives, are tranquillised by patriarchal psychiatrists and defined as mad.

The institutions of the patriarchal State are as damaging to the material existence and potential of human beings as the threat or reality of physical violence which comes from the barrel of a gun. At one end of the spectrum, the violence of the State can be seen through its repressive agents, the armed forces and police, and at the other the violence reverberates painfully — if sometimes imperceptibly — throughout our homes, schools and personal relationships. Feminism's major contribution has been to locate the 'personal' within the political arena. In order to change these oppressive and violent economic and social relationships we have to start to change ourselves. We cannot fight for peace and ignore the violence on the streets and in our homes; we cannot successfully confront the violence of our everyday lives without struggling for total change.

CHAPTER 2

Breaking the Chains

Nonviolence

What exactly is nonviolence? It is much more than simply an absence of violence. It is both a principle and a technique, a set of ideas about how life should be lived and a strategy for social change. Respect for life is a fundamental feature, together with the desire for liberation. This means not deliberately killing, hurting, threatening or putting fear into others, in short, not treating them as less human than ourselves. When respect for life and desire for liberation are made into guidelines for political action, they say a great deal. In order to translate these values into strategic tactics, the goals sought and the methods adopted need to be consistent. Indeed, this is where nonviolence parts company with many other approaches to social change. Having liberation as a goal necessarily implies that you prize a fuller and freer life for everyone and that is what is important.

Why then can't you establish a loving, caring, plentiful and satisfying society by using a bit of intimidation, deceit, injustice, terror and murder? It should be obvious that you can't, and the short answer is that these kinds of methods will simply bear their own fruit. The Red Army Fraction (Baader-Meinhof group) used violent means which led to no discernible improvement, nor any hope of it, in West German society. In fact, not only did it result in the torture and murder of its own members, but it also resulted in a general crackdown on political activists throughout West Germany. Although we were in sympathy with the general aims for political change of the Red Army Fraction, we could not support their means.

But there are times when we are more sympathetic towards the use of violence, when the choices are severely restricted and any move towards change is hope for the future, even though we know that violence breeds violence. For example, when Verwoerd, the Prime Minister of South Africa, was killed in 1966, we hoped that the repressive apartheid regime would be at last relaxed, although we regretted the violence of the murder. The fact is, however, that it did not improve the lot of black and coloured South Africans, while the predictable increase in police powers, raids and harassment did take place. However, nonviolent methods are not guaranteed to protect us from violence, as is shown by the brutal death in custody of Steve Biko, who was committed to nonviolent struggle.

You don't need to be an advanced political thinker to see how one injustice leads to another; no country has yet fought the war to end all wars. Rather than getting to the roots of the problems, killing and violence only pose it in another way.

Conflict and how to deal with it is central to nonviolence. Many people have an idea of nonviolence as avoiding conflict at all costs but it has to be stressed that nonviolence is much more 'worldly' than its image. It assumes what the American nonviolent feminist Barbara Deming calls 'the importance of active involvement in conflict and of involving oneself in social situations and wielding power responsibly'. So we try not to duck issues but to involve ourselves in them. We don't threaten our opponents nor, by extension, are we willing to rely on others to do it for us. That's why we are active in the struggles against nuclear reactors, policies that create mass unemployment, massive military budgets and factory farming. It also means that we do not want to rely on the armed forces as our 'defenders' nor on sophisticated weapons systems capable of mass destruction.

Obviously when Barbara Deming talks of 'wielding power responsibly', she is not referring to power as it is wielded by those in positions of power today. That kind of power is always 'power over', power to dominate, terrorise, or oppress. Nonviolence is, rather, about abolishing power as we know it and redefining it as something common to all, to be used by all and for all. Power over is to be replaced by shared power, by the power to do things, by the discovery of our own strength as opposed to a passive receiving of power exercised by others, often in our name. Individuals feel, and in many ways *are* powerless against 'the authorities', but we are more than individuals; we can find strength, confidence and real power in working together. Trying to find and build on common struggles and common interests is practising nonviolence.

Though the individual, such as a conscientious objector, can express an active nonviolence, it is by working together that we can be most effective. Essential to nonviolence, too, is the belief that everyone can do it, that each person regardless of gender, colour, class, age or physical abilities has a vital part to play in any nonviolent movement. This contrasts with some assumptions of violent struggle, such as guerilla warfare, whose aims of liberation may be the same as any nonviolent struggle, but whose methods exclude a very large number of the people they are aiming to liberate, such as women with dependents, old people, children, etc. Because these people are excluded from participation in the fight, they tend to be excluded from the decisions, and change can take place in their name but outside their control. Nonviolent resistance

Nonviolent direct action was an important part of the nuclear disarmament movement in the 1950s and sixties. Here members of the Direct Action Committee Against Nuclear War attempt to obstruct the supply ship for US Polaris nuclear submarines in the Holy Loch, Scotland.

can involve risks which make some kinds of activities difficult for some people, but the success of any struggle depends on involvement in many different ways and everyone's contribution is equally valid and essential to the kind of society we hope to create.

Within our study group there has been much debate about the extent to which guerilla warfare, as part of a war of liberation against intolerable oppression, conflicts with our notion of the effectiveness and morality of nonviolent methods. Barbara Deming, in *Revolution and Equilibrium,* echoes the sentiments of some of us: 'Can you call degrading the violence used by the oppressed to throw off oppression? When one is confronted . . . with the "violence of the status quo" — conditions which are damaging, even murderous, to very many who must live within them — it is degrading for all to allow such conditions to persist. And if the individuals who can find the courage to bring about change see no way in which it can be done without employing violence on their own part — a much lesser violence, they feel, than the violence to which they will put an end — I do not feel that I can judge them. The judgements I make are not judgements upon people but on the means open to us. What are the best means for changing our lives — for really changing them?'

We also realise that it is dangerous to make judgements about political actions in distant countries, when the only information we receive is through the mass media of which we are otherwise totally sceptical. We therefore try to find out, listen to, and trust the judgements of those involved in fighting for their freedom. Father Gasper Garcia Laviana is one such voice which gives us some guidance on the situation in Nicaragua: 'I'd seen perhaps the most miserable, the most oppressed of Niacargua. I tried to respond in a Christian way, peacefully, promoting social and human development . . . But I realised it was all a lie, all deceit. I became discouraged to see that so much work had meant nothing, that so many hopes were left in the air. The people continued living the same . . . And so I joined the armed struggle, knowing that nothing peaceful was possible . . . any other way would have been dishonest to my people and myself.' (From *Nicaragua* by Susan Meiselas.) The emergence of the State of Zimbabwe from white minority rule was brought about by years of armed struggle which eventually forced the white rulers (British and Rhodesian) to the negotiating table. The ending of white rule and the setting up of Zimbabwe based on majority rule involved the liberation of millions, and was therefore undoubtedly to be welcomed.

Thus in working for the eradication of the greatest evil we may find ourselves temporarily allied with some very different approaches. These may be guerilla movements, the armed forces, as in Portugal in the left wing revolution of 1974 or the police — concerned at Luxulyan, Cornwall, that protestors also have rights and that it was not the job of the police to act as bully boys for the Central Electricity Generating Board on private land.

Yet we still have a commitment not to mirror the behaviour and methods of an oppressive system. It is not enough to denounce violence everywhere as if it were something clear-cut and equally dreadful in every situation; the point is somehow, and permanently, to reduce it and the damage it does.

By not avoiding conflicts, nonviolence means a willingness to take personal risks and, at times, to bear suffering without retaliation. Although we accept the practical limitations discussed above, our goal is always to make our means consistent with the ends, believing that a just society will be born from peaceful means. Nonviolence does not say that nobody gets hurt, that violence won't be meted out to us, nor that the last vestiges of institutionalised violence are going to be given up without a fight. But it *does* say that real lasting changes can be made in this way, and that in the long term fewer people, and other forms of life, will be destroyed.

Nonviolent methods of action for social change have been the subject of many manuals, and, undoubtedly, preparation and nonviolent action training play an enormous part in spreading the

29

ideas and building that confidence in our own 'power to . . .'. There is no room here for details of civil disobedience, non-co-operation, organising a meeting or a picket, joint decision making or direct action. Suffice it to say that the methods chosen are those which are most likely to achieve the goals set in a manner consistent with them — methods that aim to include others, to de-escalate violence, to get to the roots of the conflict and not to forget the humanity of our opponents. A basic principle of nonviolent theory is that our real opponent is not the police constable who hits us on a demonstration, but the system which creates their job and arms them with the authority to oppress.

Nonviolent methods also make sense in purely practical terms. It's not feasible for us to beat 'them' at their own game as we don't have the weapons of repression, and those in power can always muster superior force from somewhere. The strength of nonviolence lies in the fact that we do not rely on leaders and elites but on the courage and determination of ordinary people to begin to run their own lives and to work for a world where this is possible for everyone.

MARGARET MURRAY

Training is an important part of preparing for nonviolent direct action. Here women enact arrest at a workshop held before the blockade of Upper Heyford airbase, Oxfordshire, New Year's Eve 1982.

Feminism

The Women's Liberation Movement, of which the Feminism and Nonviolence Study Group is an active part, has formulated the following demands:

We assert the right of every woman to a self-defined sexuality, and demand

1. Equal pay
2. Equal education and job opportunities
3. Free contraception and abortion on demand
4. Free 24-hour nurseries, under community control
5. Legal and financial independence
6. An end to discrimination against lesbians
7. Freedom from intimidation by the threat or use of violence or sexual coercion, regardless of marital status. An end to the laws, assumptions and institutions that perpetuate male dominance and men's aggression towards women.

These are a basic minimum, to which we add many more requirements for our liberation, such as shared domestic responsibility, the ending of abuse by the media, and appropriate and adequate health care for women. The invisibility of women's oppression is proof of its all pervasiveness. Our suffering seems so normal that it becomes invisible. The restrictions and degradations are so entrenched that they have acquired a timeless quality which makes them appear natural and immutable. But this is not so, the system has been constructed over the centuries by laws and institutions that were developed by men and which, until very recently, excluded women. If women had ever had any power in the formation of these structures, less oppressive conditions might have prevailed.

Feminists want not only an end to these patterns of oppression, but to do away with the power and mentality that once produced and now maintain them. We recognise that there are also groups of men excluded from the power structure — black, working class or gay men — with whom we share the bottom rungs of the social ladder.

Such is the insidious nature of oppression that we too have taken in the messages about how and what we ought to be. It would be difficult to remain untouched by pop records, magazines, television and journalism. Not surprisingly we often do still think of ourselves as inferior, feel awful about not conforming to unattainable physical stereotypes, don't have any confidence in our own achievements and so on. So both women and men have a lot of rethinking to do; we have to question all our ideas once we accept that women are oppressed.

We have to ask which of our ideas about the ordering of society are still valid and how we intend to approach changing things.

VALERIE WILMER

The struggle for equal pay continues: the National Coal Board pays male canteen workers the same as surface workers, while women who do the same work earn much less.

Liberation is not just a change of viewpoint, but begins with a long hard look at how we are. Not all feminists are agreed about 'how we are' and thus how change is to come about. What we are agreed on is that each woman has it in her own power to start to make some changes in her life, that she has more to give and to receive than she was ever allowed to believe. We know that domination and abuse of power should be things of the past. So feminists assert the value of moving away from competition and ambition for personal gain towards autonomous organisation, egalitarian structures and the importance of sharing skills, information and ideas.

These are values supposedly striven for but rarely achieved in the traditional left. What feminists have added is a profound and revolutionary understanding that nothing that happens in our personal lives is without a meaning in public life, that it has something to say about society as a whole. In other words, the personal is political. Feminists have put political emphasis on the importance of supporting each other through the difficult steps towards changing our lives. To realise that we have the power to start to control some aspects of our own lives is an exhilarating and liberating feeling.

Women's liberation challenges not only women's position in the ordering of society, but the very assumptions upon which it is based. Lesbianism challenges the assumption of heterosexuality in men and women. The control of women's bodies by theological and medical 'experts' is challenged by the demand for free abortion on demand. The availability of women's bodies is challenged by our organising against pornography and by helping women who have been raped. Women now question the values that sons and daughters are supposed to acquire; the nuclear family is challenged by women who refuse to take on the 'owned' status of the married woman and by those who decide not to seek fulfilment through motherhood. But because these subjects are so challenging, demanding real changes of both women and men, feminists are often deliberately misunderstood and the problems trivialised.

When women group together to work for peace and disarmament we are often portrayed as expressing our true nature, since women are said to be 'guardians of life on earth'. On the contrary, we are politically motivated and very angry people, angry on our own behalf.

PAM ISHERWOOD

33

Feminist Nonviolence

'I am convinced that the truest act of courage, the strongest act of manliness is to sacrifice ourselves for others in a totally nonviolent struggle for justice. To be a man is to suffer for others. God help us to be men.' (Cesar Chavez, leader of the United Farm Workers Union in the US struggling for the rights of migrant workers, March 1968.)

Even allowing for the varieties of nonviolence and the different strands of feminism, it should be easy to see how they would blend well together. In both, liberation is of primary importance, along with belief in the strength of each individual, an abhorrence of domination and hierarchy, the reassertion of the importance of feelings, the openness to change ourselves and a concern for all forms of life. Clearly nonviolence would not be acceptable, as a principled position, to those feminists who believe that men will not, indeed cannot, change. Their vision of the future has no place for men, other than a very subservient one. Men would have to be held back from *any* positions they might abuse.

We believe however that the nonviolent society for which we are working would aspire not to be oppressive in any way. We accept that, despite difficulties, men have to be part of the solution if they are not to continue to be part of the problem. In the meantime we try not to let men drain the energy we have for other women and we work with men on our terms. Women have been men's source of inspiration, consolation and energy for thousands of years; we are due centuries of 'energy credit'.

Some of us in the group came to the peace movement through feminism, and some of us came to the women's liberation movement through the peace movement. Now we all find it hard to tease the two apart and allocate ideas to one or other source. However, there are points where our feminism comes into conflict with male-defined notions of nonviolence: the questions of women's invisibility as political activists, self-defence, abortion, holding onto the value of nurturing and de-escalating conflict without being seen as 'traditionally feminine'.

It is often argued that abortion is killing and thus not consistent with nonviolent ideas. As feminists we also look to the violence done to the woman who is made to have a child against her will, including, often, conception against her will. We look at the question in the context of male sexual domination, of death by backstreet abortionists, at the deaths of thousands of women . . . and there can be no doubt that we demand the woman's right to choose.

The well-spring of some of these differences is the fact that many of the revered nonviolent theorists have been men, whilst many of the practitioners have been women. Most of these men were members of an oppressed race — Gandhi, Martin Luther King,

Cesar Chavez — but they had one thing in their favour — being men. 'We know that however much they may think they are writing about human experience, men are describing a world they have seen through the eyes of the privileged. We are right to be cautious. We must not accept, even for a moment, male notions of what nonviolence is,' wrote the US feminist writer Andrea Dworkin.

So how is traditional nonviolence 'male-defined'? Firstly, by refusing to take women's oppression as seriously as other causes — uranium mining, Northern Ireland, racism, Third World, nuclear weapons, animal liberation — almost anything in the repertoire of respectable causes for political activists to embrace. None of these is greeted with the trivialisation and ridicule that can still greet feminism. The oppression of women can be regarded as the prime model, it's the one boys learn first. As Andrea Dworkin wrote: 'Any commitment to nonviolence which is real, which is authentic, must begin in the recognition of the forms and degrees of violence perpetrated against women by the gender class men. Any analysis of violence or commitment to act against it, that does not begin there is hollow, meaningless — a sham which will have as its direct consequence, the perpetuation of our servitude.'

We want to look at one of the problems arising from the male definition of nonviolence, one which has a bearing on the theoretical problem at the root of many of them — the importance of *seeking out* suffering.

> According to the science of Satyagraha (nonviolent resistance), the greater the repression and lawlessness on the part of authority, the greater should be the suffering courted by the victims. Success is the certain result of suffering of the extremest character voluntarily undergone. (Letter from Gandhi to the Viceroy, 8/5/30)
>
> My personal trials have also taught me the value of unmerited suffering. As my suffering mounted I soon realised that there were two ways I could respond to my situation — either to react with bitterness or seek to transform the suffering into a creative force. I decided to follow the latter course. Recognising the necessity of suffering, I have tried to make of it a virtue. (Martin Luther King in *Strength to Love*)

This suffering had a deep religious significance and a spiritual value independent of any practical, worldly, tactical value. That apart, it was seen as a tool for use here and now. However it does not always work like that. The total number of person hours of suffering does not lead 'automatically' to an equivalent amount of success.

Kampuchea and Chile would be heaven on earth by now if that were so. These men are talking about voluntary suffering, with the assumption that its value lies in its being sought — resulting in an extra, shocking and visible impact.

For women, however, physical and emotional suffering is rarely sought, it is already much more a part of mere existence. Women are battered, sexually abused, do 60 per cent of the world's work and own less than 10 per cent of the world's wealth. Thus women's suffering carries less of the visibility and moral virtue. The presence of women at Greenham Common peace camp has commonly resulted in media coverage concentrating on 'the family left to cope at home' whilst playing down the hardships of the women who camped out during one of England's harshest winters.

Moreover should we not be cautious of men telling us that suffering is a good thing? Would Gandhi have accepted that from the British or Martin Luther King from the whites? No, the point is that it is we alone who can decide how much we are prepared to pay in each case for the cause in question. Emily Davison laid down her life for women's suffrage when she threw herself under the King's horse at the Derby in 1913, though it is not clear that this significantly furthered the cause. We too are prepared to suffer but we don't seek it out as something valuable in itself: to do so, we feel is a form of machismo.

Often the values and practice of nonviolence overlap with what could be called 'traditional female qualities', which isn't surprising since they are both outside the dominant culture, that based on 'traditional male qualities'. The danger is that in confronting our conditioning we will discard much that is actually positive, simply because society ascribes it to women. In this way the methods and values of nonviolence, with its connotations of acquiescence and passivity, could be rejected too, since in patriarchal terms, they do not seem to be steps towards our liberation.

To continue to be concerned for the welfare of others, to refuse to use physical violence to get what we want — these may be 'traditional female qualities' and thus under scrutiny by the Women's Liberation Movement. We are still working towards an understanding of what we can make *our* definition. The understanding of nonviolence as activity rather than passivity does link with feminist efforts to encourage women to be more assertive. Thus we feel that we are at the beginning of working out a definition, a theory and a practice of feminist nonviolence.

CHAPTER 3

Claiming Our Lives

Refusing To Be Victims

How we respond to violence depends very much on the kind of violence with which we are confronted. It depends, too, on how best we are able to intervene effectively in any situation. Effective nonviolence does mean intervention, whether it is blocking lorries bringing supplies to build a Cruise missile base, moving in to calm down a street fight at closing time or simply suggesting a way of resolving an argument at a meeting. Someone committed to nonviolence tries to find a solution which will be most constructive for most people, though not necessarily at the least risk to themselves. It is a commitment to activity, not passivity.

In some senses the 'bigger' the objective and the more of us working for it, the more irrelevant violent tactics can become. To make the British government realise that it will have to get rid of nuclear weapons will take the organised might of the vast mass of people in this country. Campaigning for that by a few people bombing air force bases would be more likely to lead to hardening attitudes in the government, increased repression of all activists and to deterring the vast majority of people from involvement, whether because they felt that violence was incompatible with the aims of disarmament or because such action could not be related to their everyday lives.

At another level, the violence of a State which expects people to live on less than £20 a week because they can't find work is obvious. The answer is not to jump the counter and hit the clerk next time you sign on: she or he is not personally responsible for that structural violence and things are more likely to change by organising with other claimants and getting the clerk to involve her/his union in campaigning for a benefits rise. Nor, if we believe in the possibility of every one to change, do we have to kill the bosses to overthrow capitalism: effective class struggle has to do with changing the property and power relations between classes not with lining up all the individuals within a class and shooting them dead.

There are times when it is hard to find an active response to violence which is nonviolent, and this is nearly always when the individual faces a situation they have not chosen, and often alone.

While we can undertake actions which might lead to being jailed or beaten up or even killed because we have freely chosen to oppose war or social injustice, we will not let ourselves be beaten up, raped or killed simply because we are women who have chosen to live with a man or to walk down a street at night. We reject violence, but we also reject collusion with violence — we refuse, where we can, to be victims.

One of the greatest problems facing victims is to become visible to their oppressors, to make them hear the sound their fist makes striking vulnerable flesh, smell the fear they inspire, feel the pain for the reality it is, and to do this without encouraging sadistic instincts. Part of the key is to organise, and much of   the work of the women's liberation movement has been just this kind of organisation against violence, as we outline further on. The purpose of this kind of organisation is not only very practical, in the support we give each other as women, but it serves to show men — and more importantly other women — that we refuse to continue as victims. An individual woman facing a violent man still confronts the problem of what she as an individual will do (take it, fight back, leave) but her choice is made easier if she knows that other women share her experience, that she is visible and what is happening is wrong. As long as individual women at home or on the streets face violence without a very active support to stop that violence, we assert the right to defend ourselves from that victimisation, including physically if necessary. The basis of most women's self defence is precisely defence — not hurting, maiming, degrading or killing our attackers but talking, shouting, running and only if necessary hitting.

Those who criticise this self defence as violence should be sure that they always intervene to prevent such violence, even in so-called 'domestic' situations, and sure too that they might never need to do the same.

We are committed to nonviolence, but our aim is liberation. If being voluntary victims, if passive suffering, if taking it like a woman could of itself liberate, millions of women would now be free. In order to change the world we must first become visible, and that means standing up and standing together.

Women Act Against Violence

The Women's Liberation Movement (WLM) has always concerned itself with struggling against male violence, analysing attacks by men not as isolated acts committed by individuals but as the vanguard of the collective male assault on all women in our society. Many feminists may have been slow to make connections between male attacks on women and male attacks on each other, on the environment and on the continued existence of our planet, but our work against violence cannot be discounted by the nonviolent movement, as it has been for too long, apparently because it has not always been consciously nonviolent.

While there are a few feminists who believe we can best defeat male violence by returning comparable acts of aggression, most feminist ways of organising incorporate, albeit unintentionally, many of the elements of a nonviolent approach to revolutionary change. These ways are based on the belief that all participants are a significant part of the action, and so protest is geared towards enabling the most people to join in and thus increase their consciousness, rather than using a dominant elite (whether physically stronger, ideologically 'sounder', less tied by domestic commitments or whatever) to do the job for us. There are many other ways, too, in which feminist and nonviolent methods of organising run parallel — sharing of skills and organisational tasks, decentralised decision-making and the breaking down of hierarchical structures. Working in nonhierarchical ways doesn't mean we never delegate decisions. Even when we entrust decision making to one or two people because of their time, energy or relevant experience, they still remain accountable to the group and aren't allowed to have power over the rest of the group in the traditional hierarchical way.

Until recently, feminists have been unwilling to look at nonviolence as a political issue. This may have been because of our need to dissociate ourselves firmly from previous male stereotypes of women's suitable revolutionary position — if not prone, at least placid — so that some feminists dismiss nonviolence even while our primary campaigns are directed against violence. Our attitude is probably also related to our experiences of men in the nonviolent movement, whose theory for defeating structural violence may be impeccable, but whose personal behaviour often remains as violent as any other man's. At least one feminist, active in the peace movement, has remarked on the irony that she has been hit more times in her life by so-called nonviolent men than by policemen or soldiers.

As nonviolent feminists we have watched a growing acceptance within the WLM that individual men attacking individual women is one end of the continuum of violence which leads inexorably to the international military abuse of power. It is not surprising that this recognition has come to many women simultaneously with the blatant international escalation of preparations for nuclear war and the growth of a global protest movement to counteract it. Men in the peace movement are only too happy to accept this new input of female energy into what they previously saw as 'their' struggle, but they often ignore the roots of this militancy, for to acknowledge the development of an independent feminist analysis of violence must mean a re-examination of their own behaviour. What we are aiming for is an integration of the two critiques of violence, and, if we are not to be drowned in the male definitions of where the struggle against violence should be primarily located, we must examine the history of the feminist struggles against violence to ensure that they are not undervalued or ignored in the struggles to come.

Perhaps the most well-known and earliest feminist campaign against violence is the network of refuges for battered women, known in Britain as Women's Aid. The first Women's Aid refuge was started in Chiswick in 1971 by Erin Pizzey, but the development of a feminist network only took off after the opening of the next refuge in Brixton in 1973. By 1975 there were about eighty Women's Aid groups around Britain, some with operating refuges,

PAM ISHERWOOD

Reclaim the Night demonstration to protest at £2000 fine imposed on a rapist by a judge who accused the woman of 'contributory negligence' by hitch-hiking at night.

some still only at the planning stage. The working of each refuge has been determined locally by the group running it, so that some discrepancies in policy have arisen, but the vast majority continue to subscribe to the vital feminist guiding principles, laid down by Brixton, that no men are allowed into the premises or onto the organising group and that, even where there are paid workers, the refuge is run as collectively as possible by the women who stay there. This ties in with two important and distinctive principles which feminists adopt in our political attack on male violence. Firstly, women refuse the definition of victim, by offering collective support and analysis with other women who have had similar experiences. Secondly, it is assumed that each woman will retain control over her own destiny, taking responsibility for her own decisions, even under extremely oppressive circumstances.

These two principles inform nearly all feminist initiatives against violence, especially those which, by their nature, have as their starting point violence against individual women which must then be integrated into a general political analysis. As well as Women's Aid, we would include in this category Rape Crisis Centres, the first one of which started in London in 1976 and of which there is now a network of about a dozen round the country; Incest Survivors Groups, which have mostly started in the last year and which contribute another vital element to our understanding of patriarchal violence by focussing on sexual attacks on young women within the family; and feminists working to defeat sexual harassment at work, often by means of women's groups within trade unions.

In November 1977, the British WLM instigated another historic action against male violence, for on one night, simultaneously in a dozen cities round the country, women gathered for the first great Reclaim the Night demonstrations, torchlit processions which erupted joyously and noisily round the streets, with painted faces and banshee wailing. We proclaimed 'All women should be free to walk down any street night or day without fear' — a modest enough demand, yet potentially very threatening to the status quo. This was confirmed when, as part of the gathering momentum of protest against violence, the third march around Soho, on Halloween 1978, was attacked by police and sixteen women were arrested. There had been many political mass arrests before — of black people, of nuclear disarmament protesters, even of other feminists — but this was the first time that many women had been confronted with state violence, especially in the ironic context of an action *against* violence that had been organised explicitly to be peaceful, if noisy. Consequently these arrests and the publicity surrounding them were very significant in helping to draw attention to the different yet connected aspects of violence against women.

They came a few months after we had adopted the seventh demand of the Women's Liberation Movement at our last national conference: Freedom from intimidation by the threat or use of violence (full list in previous chapter). Perhaps the addition of this demand, followed by the Soho 16 arrests, could be seen as the consolidation of a form of unarticulated nonviolent analysis which has characterised much of feminist politics. The seventh demand uncompromisingly makes demands of men, as individuals and in groups, rather than only of the State, that oppressive yet nebulous institution for which no one has to accept ultimate personal responsibility. At the same time, when discussing the wording, we rejected overwhelmingly words which would have committed us to supporting women defending themselves *by any means possible.* In practice, there would be few occasions when feminists would not support a woman defending herself against male attack, but to have supported that wording could have been seen as an open invitation to escalate female-initiated aggression. Struggling against violence seems to be one area of feminist activity where the most positive form of action is not seen as providing a female alternative to male practices, but rather as the necessity of exposing them and defeating them wherever they occur.

Since 1980 many of these strands of the Women's Liberation Movement's struggle against male violence have come together under the umbrella of WAVAW, Women Against Violence Against Women. This network not only organises against direct assaults on our bodies, but also against more insidious forms of violence, such as pornography. From previously having seen pornography as a means of stimulating men into thinking and acting in violent ways, many women now feel that pornography is itself another form of violence. As there are now several videos on sale in the high streets of this country which show women actually being murdered, this seems to be increasingly true.

Lately 'Angry Women' have burned and vandalised porn shops in several places making it clear that their attacks are on property and not on people. Without condemning such attacks we feel doubtful about the place of such tactics in a traditional definition of nonviolent action. Although with all good intention they are meant to be an unambiguous attack on property and not on people, it is not so clear that somebody won't get hurt. Arson attacks are risky, both in terms of the heavy charges to the arsonists if caught, and also because of the uncertainty that nobody will get hurt by the fire. They could provide an excuse for an escalation in violence against women involved with other feminist activities, and unlike some other actions involving damage to property — for example, the destruction of cinema screens showing pornography — arson is unlikely to win over people to the campaign.

When looking at the Women's Liberation Movement's response to violence, it is a shock to realise that it is not only those feminist campaigns which fight explicitly against violence which must be examined, but it is clear that almost any struggle against the patriarchy is a struggle against male violence. Whether the feminist campaign is in the area of physical or mental health, about being black or a lesbian, a prostitute or a homeworker, we are constantly having to struggle against being tortured and brutalised with male tools of control, whether drugs or electric shocks, pins or pricks, operating knives or flick knives or just plain dirty money.

This is structural violence at its most profound, and it is time for men to realise that they are responsible for it, and that as women we have been struggling against it for many years and will carry on doing so until it is defeated on all levels. Our struggle is particularly essential in defeating those kinds of violence which are designed to isolate women from each other, making us feel individually inadequate, and which above all are designed to perpetuate power relationships where the man is, literally or metaphorically, on top.

TIM MALYON

43

Women and the Peace Movement

In Britain many political movements — not just feminism — have incorporated nonviolent methods into their approaches, usually without being explicit. Where nonviolence has been applied, it's been in connection with a specific event rather than being the philosophical basis for a movement. The occupation of the reactor site at Torness, the siege of another site at Luxulyan, stopping the seal cull, the despatch of the boat Rainbow Warrior against whalers, erecting scaffolding to stop a nuclear waste train at Sharpness and the Greenham Common peace camp are all examples of such actions. So we cannot examine the actions of the 'nonviolent movement' as such, though we can look at the peace movement which exemplifies many of our views, but has not as yet developed an explicit nonviolent approach nor a thorough critique of violence. We have also increasingly felt that the peace movement is relegating 'women's issues' to consideration 'after the weapons issues'. This is not good enough.

There is an assumption in the peace movement that men in it are somehow different from other men and therefore exempt from oppressive behaviour and sexism. Alas, women working in mixed 'broad-based' peace groups have found that this is not always the case. Although groups work differently, many women have found problems working in them which are usually related to the men's political working traditions as well as more 'personal' difficulties of working with men. At one extreme, some groups have hardly heard of 'women's lib', don't expect women to contribute much and are dominated by the chairman or a few vocal, confident members. More sophisticated groups waste hours on sectarian in-fighting, ego-tripping and internal political arguments.

Very little time is ever given to the doubts and fear of people who are trying to deal with the possibility of annihilation, to the consideration of new ways of working to break down that fear and paralysis or to the problems of people joining the peace movement who are new to political activity and easily alienated by lack of explanation, in-jokes and traditional, unquestioned forms of political activity. Some groups have tried to become more democratic, but a common sense of urgency about *the* issue often prevents work on genuinely trying to make sure that everyone can participate, thus making the groups more effective.

A tendency to glorify certain sorts of activism goes hand in hand with the assumption that men are more likely to be free of domestic responsibilities and therefore able to undertake these activities, with a consequent down-grading of other forms of commitment. Basic to feminism is the idea that everyone's contribution is important and valid: we reject the kind of 'alternative machismo' (expounded by some women as well as men in the peace movement)

44

which assesses people's commitment on the basis of how often they resist arrest or go to jail. The success of a broad-based popular struggle, like that for peace, depends on many different sorts of involvement (addressing envelopes, leafleting the high street, running the creche as well as occupying air-bases). The value of any action depends on how effective it is, not on how many people get arrested.

Some women have acquired the confidence (often class-based) to speak up in meetings, but our role generally is still often one of mediators and of background workers quietly doing the hard slog and detailed work behind any event. It is a long, slow process trying to carry over into mixed peace groups some of the lessons learned in the Women's Liberation Movement about the participation and validation of all members and all contributions, and it is all too easy for women's creativity and energy to be sapped by the struggle to communicate these lessons.

However, women have started to organise separately within and outside the peace movement, just as they have with every other movement for social change over the last ten years or so. Inevitably cries of 'divisiveness' are heard, as we are accused of weakening the struggle just when we most need a united human front. In fact, the founders of that much-respected organisation, the Women's International League for Peace and Freedom (WILPF), were apparently busy being divisive back in 1915, before any of the current mixed peace organisations came into being. In a society where women daily suffer humiliation, slights, undermining of confidence and often physical violence in the attempt to keep us in

STEVE RAPPORT

45

our place, organising together can be the only way of strengthening us and giving us the necessary courage to get out of it! We understand the sense of urgency that permeates the peace movement — it is also our own — but we need to recognise that many women will not survive *today,* let alone in the future for which we are working.

Independent women's groups have already made a significant contribution to the peace movement, notably the women who have camped at Greenham Common since September 1981 who have provided inspiration and a model for the numerous peace camps that have sprung up since, in Britain and abroad. Women Oppose the Nuclear Threat (WONT) is rooted firmly in the Women's Liberation Movement but exists, too, as part of the peace movement. Its commitment to the anti-nuclear struggle stems from a feminist analysis of the arms race and of the militarism that is threatening the planet. Clearly, the Women's Liberation Movement over the last twelve years has made it easier for women within the peace movement to organise together, to be conscious of our role *as women* within it and to have a critique of the causes of militarism.

However, we also see some distinct differences within the peace movement between feminists and those women who see a distinctive place for women but on the basis of our traditional role. The argument comes out along the lines: 'Men have made a mess of the world; women are going to save it. Our planet needs love and nurturance — as mothers we know about that.' This is a short step to the idea that women are *naturally* co-operative, peaceful, caring and nurturing (precisely the same idea that the government is trying to use to disguise the fact that women are being forced out of paid work and back into the home as unpaid carers, nurses and community volunteers). This sounds dangerously close to the notion that 'biology is destiny' — an idea which has been consistently used to keep women down.

Whilst there is no doubt that the qualities of caring and nurturance that most women learn from our infancy are crucial to the development of the human community, we should be insisting that *men* learn precisely these qualities, not that our role in the peace movement is to exemplify them. Appealing to women as 'Mothers' relieves men of the responsibility for becoming carers, nurturers, co-operative, whilst belittling women who aren't biological mothers, either by choice or by necessity. Families against the Bomb is a classic example of women falling into these traps; whilst it might seem reasonable to try to reach women who might identify with such a name, it totally fails to see the assumptions behind it. Both 'Families against the Bomb' and 'Babies against the Bomb' involve women who refuse to put themselves as women first, preferring to identify primarily with

46

Organised by women, the demonstration at Greenham Common airbase in December 1982 attracted 30,000 women to embrace the base on the 12th — third anniversary of the decision to site Cruise missiles in Europe — while 3,000 blockaded the base the next day.

The Greenham Common Women's Peace Camp, set up in September 1981, has helped inspire many peace camps in Britain and other parts of Europe. 'Comiso doesn't want to become tomorrow's Hiroshima' says the banner brought from the Comiso peace camp, Sicily, to Greenham Common.

families and babies. Both Families and Babies against the Bomb serve to 'hide' the women who organise demos and lobbies in their name, as well as exploiting babies who are given no choice in the matter. Instead, their vulnerability, their newness, their precarious future, are used to appeal to popular and sentimental notions about babies and motherhood. Finally, the very title serves to trivialise other autonomous groups who *choose* to come together within the peace movement from a common base — disabled or gay people, for example.

There is plenty of evidence, too, that the Women-as-Natural-Peacemakers school of thought is mistaken: the qualities of caring and nurturance that many women exemplify (and that, shorn of their enforced and conditioned nature, are of course crucial to society) are not innate at all. Women have on occasion been notoriously brutal — witness Nazi death camp women guards — and in positions of authority can be as sadistic as any man. Women may be less likely to get into fights or be convicted of violent offences, but we do sometimes fight, each other and men, on the streets, in pubs and discos. Because, too, definitions of violence are limited, other female behaviour, such as depression, is not perceived as violence, with the woman herself as the main victim.

It is most important that we do not see our role within the peace movement primarily as mothers and carers. It can be a tempting way of persuading women to become politically active, but it also relieves men of their responsibility for transforming themselves, developing caring human qualities, for being responsible for childcare and housework and all other essential support work. Children are not just the responsibility of their biological mothers and we are *all* responsible for the future of the planet. Defining women primarily as nurturers limits our role within the peace movement and within the world. It is very easy to lose sight of this when so many people are feeling that the earth itself is on the verge of extermination, but this sense of urgency should not blind us to the vision of the kind of world that we want to build, nor to our day-to-day struggle against those forces that continually seek to diminish or destroy us.

BRENDA PRINCE

Spinning and weaving are traditional images of women's creativity. The Women's Pentagon Actions in the USA in 1980 and 1981 used wool to obstruct the Pentagon as women here at Upper Heyford use it to link to each other and the airbase.

CHAPTER 4

A Time to Come

One of the things we have hoped to do with this pamphlet is to raise awareness in the peace movement of both the ideas and practices of feminism and nonviolence. While we see occasional conflicts between feminism and nonviolence as it has been defined, there is an overlapping approach between them which presents great possibilities for the growth and strengthening of the peace movement as a whole. In particular, many of the organisational practices can be valuable for peace groups, such as finding alternatives to committees, permanent chairmen, sitting in rows in meetings, or the huge plenaries of a CND national conference. Developing ways of getting everyone to participate, discouraging interruptions and bad listening, and learning to be our own 'experts', in terms both of information gathering and trusting our own feelings, can be crucial to developing courage, initiative and imagination — all of which we will need if we are going to get disarmament.

However, though most of us are active in the peace movement, as nonviolent feminists we see that movement as only one strand in the broader movement for social change, and not in itself enough to create the kind of society we want. Other movements are also working for that change — the labour movement, the socialist parties and groups, the ecology movement, organisations working against racism, the gay movement, and the Women's Liberation Movement — and we see a need not only to participate in, but to build alliances with, these movements. While we know that we have much to learn from the experience of people in these struggles, we also feel that they can gain from a consciousness of nonviolent feminism and that what we seek is an integration of consciousness.

Because the conjunction of nonviolence and feminism is relatively new, and we ourselves feel only at the beginning of developing that synthesis, this pamphlet is concerned with theory. We feel it is important sometimes to draw breath, to take time to work out what we think, as well as to get on with the urgent work on which our survival may depend. We in this group have learned less from what we have read (though some books have inspired and clarified) than from our experience, collective and individual, in struggle. So we hope that others will see what we have written less as an end in itself than as a place to start.

Though we are often very clear about what we are struggling against, sometimes it is harder to envisage what we are struggling for. It's particularly hard to do that in a time like this, when an economic recession and its political effects mean we have to put enormous amounts of energy into keeping the little we have. Defensive struggles can make for defensive politics and it is easy to lose sight of that vision which can make all our hard work, and even our setbacks and defeats, have meaning and worth.

For us, it is impossible to separate the changes we want from the way in which we make them, so we must have a vision of the new world if we are to find the right roads to it. What follows is not a blueprint we want to impose on anyone, because the essence of our vision is that it is made collectively. We know too that changes trigger more changes, that we cannot foresee all the possibilities that will open up once some changes are made, that our children will be able to see more clearly than us. This is our sketch: you will have another, our daughters another still.

Peace means more than just an absence of war. As long as the world is divided into nation states, each competing for material wealth and political power, war is inevitable in some form or another. So, too, is the imperialist domination of weaker nation states by richer, stronger ones, whether that imperialism takes the form of actual military occupation or economic exploitation by 'agreement'. So we look forward to a time when the concept of nation has gone, when we are all equal members of the human community, sharing the resources of the world. Co-operation across frontiers already exists, with such services as the railways and the post office: we want to extend it to all aspects of life.

The State is only one possible way to organise and administer a given geographical area. We suggest the basic unit of organisation could be much smaller, so that control over the decisions which affect our lives can be made by all of us participating in non-

TIM MALYON

hierarchical organisations. Communication between these smaller units could be made easier by the modern technology of communication and information systems, which are now mainly used to oppress us. The present concentration of power at a centre from which decisions are forced upon the rest of us is a simpler form of organisation than the one we envisage, basically because the decisions come one way down a chain of command instead of being made horizontally by consensus between many equal small groups. As Alexander Berkman, an anarchist communist, put it, anarchism means organisation, more organisation, and still more organisation — so if we are all to control all the decisions we will put more time and energy into that organising than we are allowed to now. This kind of decentralisation would not happen quickly: we will all have to make personal changes to dissolve habits of domination and submission and to maintain a constant determination to devolve decision-making away from the centre.

Part of this re-organisation of power would depend on doing away with armed forces, for force is the ultimate sanction of any form of authority and each nation state depends on an army (its own or, in some cases, another State's). We will have to find some way to settle disputes between groups or people: creating a society in which there is no violence, theft or exploitation of any sort may take generations and in the meantime we will have to safeguard the weak against the strong. Again, with a strong commitment to decentralisation, we see this role as devolving mainly to the local community.

The material resources of the world will be shared equally between all the people of the world. This will mean in the first instance control of the land passing to those who live on it, the means of production of commodities to those who produce them, and control of mineral and other natural resources returning to those living where they are to be found. But it will mean more than that, for not everyone grows food or works in a factory, and the natural resources of the world are not evenly distributed geographically. So it will mean sharing these material resources on a basis of need, both between people as individuals and between what were once nations. This means inevitably that the material wealth of certain societies, such as our own in Britain, will in some ways be decreased in the interests of economic equality for the whole world.

Because the basis of the world economy will be people's needs not profits, we see an end to useless toil and the opportunity for everyone to do useful work. This doesn't mean that no work will be hard, boring, dirty or even dangerous but that such work will be shared equally, its hardship or danger minimised, and everyone will have the chance to do exciting, enjoyable or creative work. Just as it is possible in a household to share both the creative work of cooking and the 'dirty' work of cleaning the lavatory, so it is possible to share the different kinds of work needed to produce the material necessities for life, organise their fair distribution, care for children, increase our knowledge of the world and create the various forms of art which can enrich our lives. We do not want total de-industrialisation or a fantasy land of happy peasants spinning their own Laura Ashley smocks. Using the latest technologies, producing for social need, we would minimise the time spent on work and leave ourselves free for other things. The elimination of the present class system would be brought about through this redistribution of resources, of work and of political power.

With this economic and political restructuring would go the development of a reverence for the resources of the earth — nature would cease to be a woman to be raped by patriarchal greed. Instead, we would have technologies appropriate to the ecology of the world and learn to live within, rather than dominate, this fine earth of minerals, plants and animals. There would, of course, be no question of lethal energy forms like nuclear power: we would foresee the development of safe forms like wind, sea and sun power. The ferocious exploitation of animals for food and 'scientific' experiment would end.

A world of women freed from the economic, social and psychological bonds of patriarchy would be a world turned upside down, creating a possibility for the development of human potential we can hardly dream of now. Having removed the need for the family to exist as an economic unit reinforcing patriarchal power, people would be free to experiment with other ways of living. All forms of relationship based on equal respect and support would be possible. Love, now so debased by economic dependence and ideological conditioning, could finally be discovered. With the enforced divisions into sex-roles gone, people could explore free relationships regardless of age, gender or physical attributes. Children would not be pushed out to a powerless periphery as they are now. The world, in terms of machines, buildings and work, would be shaped to include the smallest, weakest and those with disabilities, not to suit only the strong.

At the same time we would all, in our own ways, become strong. With women asserting our rightful place, the qualities traditionally known as feminine — intuitive, caring and supportive — would be cultivated by us all, men and women. We would all have the opportunity to acquire those qualities said to be masculine — competence, confidence and independence — not least by giving each other the room to fail. The rich and infinite differences of people's personalities would be accepted and even cherished.

This vision could not be achieved quickly and it would not happen all at once. Nor would any part of it occur automatically as a result of another part being achieved, as Marx supposed the State would 'wither away' after power had been seized by the working class. Moreover, one part of it, for example disarmament and the dissolution of armed forces, could not be accomplished without big changes in all the other aspects of society. This is why we .are opposed to violence in all its forms: patriarchy, capitalism (including state capitalism) and the State.

Would the society we envisage be perfect? No, there would still be natural disasters, accidents and human mistakes — without the last there would be no room to grow and change. No doubt there would still be conflicts, but in a society in which everyone was committed to working things out without violence, confrontation would be seen less as a threat than a challenge: how can we solve this problem without anyone being silenced or put down, without 'win' or 'lose'? People would still sometimes be unhappy: love between individuals might be unequally returned, there would still be the anguish and searching that can make art, people reading the history of our present times might weep with compassion for our lives. There would still be death, but in a world where people's lives had not been stolen from them, where death did not come prematurely through war, starvation or murder, death would have its rightful place as the completion of a full and fruitful life, to be celebrated as much as mourned.

Utopia would be so boring, we are always told by those who have seen no vision or want to prevent us making ours real. Ask the two thirds of the world starving now whether having enough food every day would be boring? And if we had not only enough food, but enough peace, freedom and love — would that bore you?

JEREMY NICHOLL

Resources

Bibliography

Books and Pamphlets

Allen, Sanders and Wallis (eds), *Conditions of Illusion,* Feminist Books, 1974.
Rudolf Bahro, *Socialism and Survival,* Heretic Books, 1982.
Alexander Berkman, *ABC of Anarchism,* Freedom Press, 1973.
Alexander Berkman, *What is Communist Anarchism?,* Dover Publications, 1972.
Joan V. Bondurant, *Conquest of Violence,* University of California Press, 1971.
Vera Brittain, *Chronicle of Youth: War Diary, 1913-17,* Fontana, 1982.
Vera Brittain, *Testament of Friendship,* Fontana/Virago, 1980.
Vera Brittain, *Testament of Experience: the years 1925-50,* Virago/Fontana, 1979.
Vera Brittain, *Testament of Youth: 1900-25,* Virago, 1978.
Audrey Bronstein, *The Triple Struggle,* War on Want, 1982.
Susan Brownmiller, *Against Our Will,* Bantam, 1976.
Angus Calder, *The People's War,* Penguin, 1982.
Rachel Carson, *Silent Spring,* Penguin, 1965.
April Carter, David Hoggett and Adam Roberts, *Nonviolent Action: A selected bibliography,* Housmans, 1970.
Central London WAVAW Group, *WAVAW — Women Against Violence Against Women,* WAVAW, 1981.
Wendy Chapkis (ed), *Loaded Questions: Women in the Military,* Transnational Institute, 1981.
Christopher Child, *The California Crusade of Cesar Chavez,* Quaker Peace and Service, 1968.
Domatila Barrios de Chungara, *Let Me Speak! Testimony of Domatila, a Woman of the Bolivian Mines,* Stage 1, 1979.
Dick Cluster (ed), *They Should Have Served that Cup of Coffee: Seven Radicals Remember the Sixties,* South End Press, 1979.
Charlie Clutterbuck and Tim Lang, *More Than We Can Chew,* Pluto, 1982.
Cynthia Cockburn, *The Local State,* Pluto, 1977.
Virginia Coover, Ellen Deacon, Charles Esser, Christopher Moore, *Resource Manual for a Living Revolution,* New Society Press, 1977.
John Cox, *Overkill: The Story of Modern Weapons,* Penguin, 1981.
Sheryl Crown, *Hell, No, We Won't Glow: the Nonviolent Occupation of a Nuclear Power Site,* Housmans, 1979.
Mary Daly, *Gyn/Ecology,* The Women's Press, 1979.
Margaretta D'Arcy, *Tell Them Everything,* Pluto, 1981.
Barbara Deming, *Remembering Who We Are,* Frog in the Well Press, 1981.
Barbara Deming, *Revolution and Equilibrium,* Grossman Publishers, 1971.
Barbara Deming, *We Cannot Live Without Our Lives,* Grossman Publishers, 1974.
Sam Dolgoff (ed), *The Anarchist Collectives: Workers Self-Management in the Spanish Revolution 1936-39,* Black Rose Press, 1974.
Andrea Dworkin, *Our Blood,* The Women's Press, 1982.
Andrea Dworkin, *Pornography: Men Possessing Women* The Women's Press, 1981.
Andrea Dworkin, *Woman Hating,* Dutton, 1974.
Cynthia Enloe, *Ethnic Soldiers,* Penguin, 1980.
Eileen Evason, *Hidden Violence: A Study of Battered Women in Northern Ireland,* Farset Co-operative Press, 1982.
Frantz Fanon, *Black Skins, White Masks,* Grove, 1967.
Feminism and Nonviolence Study Group, *Neither Victim Nor Assassin: Feminism and Nonviolence Shrew,* 1978.
Feminist Anthology Collective (eds), *No Turning Back: Writings from the WLM 1975-1980,* The Women's Press, 1981.

Feminists Against Nuclear Power, *Nuclear Resisters,* 1981.

Leah Fritz, *Thinking Like A Woman,* WIN Books, 1975.

Mohandas Gandhi, *An Autobiography: The Story of My Experiments with Truth,* Navajivan Trust, 1927, and Penguin, 1983.

Mohandas Gandhi, *Women and Injustice,* Navajivan Trust, 1942.

Sally Gearhart, *The Wanderground,* Persephone Press, 1980.

Emma Goldman, *Living My Life* (2 vols.) Dover Publications, 1971.

Peter Grafton, *You, You and You: The People Out of Step with World War Two,* Pluto, 1982.

Susan Griffin, *Pornography and Silence,* The Women's Press, 1981.

May Hobbs, *Born to Struggle,* Quartet, 1973.

Martin Honeywell and Jenny Pearce, *Falklands/Malvinas — Whose Crisis?,* Latin America Bureau, 1982.

In and Against the State: Discussion Notes for Socialists, Pluto Press, 1980.

Martin Jelfs and Sandy Merritt, *Manual for Action,* Action Resources Group, 1982.

Lynne Jones, *Keeping the Peace,* The Women's Press, 1983.

Martin Luther King, Jr., *Why We Can't Wait,* New American Library, 1964.

Susan Koen and Nina Swaim, *Ain't Nowhere We Can Run, Handbook for Women on the Nuclear Mentality,* Women Against Nuclear Development, 1980.

Käthe Kollwitz, *Graphics, Posters and Drawings,* Writers and Readers, 1981.

Peter Kropotkin, *The Conquest of Bread,* Allen Lane, 1972.

Peter Kropotkin (ed Colin Ward), *Fields, Factories and Workshops,* George Allen and Unwin, 1974.

George Lakey, *Strategy for a Living Revolution,* Freeman, 1973.

Ursula Le Guin, *The Dispossessed,* Panther Books, 1975.

Robert Lekachman and Borin Van Loon, *Capitalism for Beginners,* Writers and Readers, 1981.

Doris Lessing, *The Marriages Between Zones Three, Four and Five,* Granada, 1981.

Linden et al (eds), *Against Sadomasochism,* Frog in the Well Press, 1982.

Manchester Law Centre, *From Ill Treatment to No Treatment, Immigration Handbook,* 1982.

Pam McAllister (ed), *Reweaving the Web of Life: Feminism and Nonviolence,* New Society Publications, 1982.

Eamonn McCann, *War and an Irish Town,* Pluto, 1980.

Arthur Marwick, *Women at War 1914-18,* Fontana, 1977.

Andrea Medea and Kathleen Thompson, *Against Rape: A Survival Manual for Women,* Peter Owen *1975.*

Medical Campaign Against Nuclear Weapons, The Medical Consequences of Nuclear Weapons, MCANW, 1982.

Susan Meiselas, *Nicaragua,* Writers and Readers, 1981.

Raynes Minns, *Bombers and Mash: The Domestic Front, 1939-45,* Virago, 1980.

Robin Morgan (ed), *Sisterhood is Powerful,* Vintage Books, 1973.

William Morris, *News from Nowhere,* Routledge, 1970.

Marge Piercy, *Woman On The Edge of Time,* The Women's Press, 1979.

Margaret Randall, *Sandino's Daughters,* Zed Press, 1982.

Catherine Reilly (ed), *Scars Upon My Heart: Women's Poetry from World War I,* Virago, 1981.

Adrienne Rich, *Compulsory Heterosexuality and Lesbian Existence,* Onlywomen Press, 1981.

Adrienne Rich, *On Lies, Secrets and Silence,* Virago, 1980.

Rosemary Radford Ruether, *New Woman New Earth,* Seabury, 1978.

Dora Russell, *The Tamarisk Tree,* Part 1. Virago, 1977, Part 2, Virago, 1981.

Gene Sharp, *The Politics of Nonviolent Action,* Vol.I, Power and Struggle, Vol. II, The Methods of Nonviolent Action, Vol.III, The Dynamics of Nonviolent Action, Porter Sargent, 1973.

Ruth Leger Sivard, *World Military and Social Expenditures — World Priorities,* WMSE Publications, annual. (Available in UK from CAAT, 5 Caledonian Road, London N1.)

Elizabeth Sigmund, *Rage Against the Dying,* Pluto, 1980.

Agnes Smedley, *Daughter of Earth,* Virago, 1977.

Leslie Tanner (ed), *Voices from Women's Liberation,* New American Library, 1971.

Dorothy Thompson (ed), *Over Our Dead Bodies — Women against the Bomb,* Virago, 1983.

E.P. Thompson and Dan Smith, *Protest and Survive*, Penguin, 1980.
Henry Thoreau, *Walden and On The Duty of Civil Disobedience*, New American
Library.
David Tinker, *A Message from the Falklands*, Penguin, 1983.
Stephanie Urdang, *Fighting Two Colonialisms: Women in Guinea-Bissau*, Monthly
Review Press, 1980.
Michelene Wandor (ed), *The Body Politic: Writings from the Women's Liberation
Movement in Britain 1969-1972*, Stage 1, 1978.
Amrit Wilson, *Finding A Voice: Asian Women in Britain*, Virago, 1978.
Gerrard Winstanley (ed Christopher Hill), *The Law of Freedom and Other
Writings*, Penguin, 1973.
Virginia Woolf, *A Room of One's Own*, Panther, 1977.
Virginia Woolf, *Three Guineas*, Penguin, 1977.

Articles

'Amazon vs Earth Mother? — Women, War and Feminism', Jean Bethke Elshtain,
The Nation, 14.6.80.
'The Army Will Make a 'Man' Out of You', Helen Michalowski, *Win*, 1.3.80.
'Aspects of NATO — Women in the Allied Forces', NATO Information Service,
1110 Brussels, March 1978.
'Changing Roles — Women in the Armed Services', Michael Cusack, *Senior
Scholastic*, 17.4.80.
Critical Social Policy, Vol.2 no.2, Autumn 1982.
'Equality in the Army — No Way', Lesley Merryfinch, *Spare Rib*, 104, March 1981.
'Feminism and Militarism: Can the Peace Movement Reach Out?', Donna
Warnock, *Win*, 15.4.82.
'"Jill Canuck": CWAC of All Trades but no "Pistol Packing Momma"', Ruth Roach
Pierson, OISE Women's Research Centre, 252 Bloor Street West, Toronto,
Ontario, Canada.
'Nuclear Power — It'll Cost the Earth', *Spare Rib,* November 1978.
'Nukes and Masculinity', Hans Enday, *Peace News*, 13.11.81.
Papers from Laurieston Hall Conference on Women and Militarism, August 1980,
from Feminism and Nonviolence Study Group.
'Sexual Divisions·and the Participation of Women in the Israeli Army', Nira
Yuval-Davis, Thames Polytechnic, Division of Sociology, 1981.
'Speak Out', Petra Kelly, *Peace News*, 13.11.81.
'Who are the Women who join the Marines?', Kathryn Marshall, *Ms*, February
1981.
'Women and Politics in Lebanon', Yolla Polity Sharara, *Khamsin* 6, Pluto Press,
1978.
'Women and the Military: a No-Win Proposition', Janis Kelly, *Off Our Backs*,
April 1980.
'Women in the Military — How are They Really Doing?', Francene Sabin,
Seventeen, July 1979.
'Women in the Nonviolent Movement', Conference Report of Les Circauds, July
1976, from War Resisters International or International Fellowship of
Reconciliation.
'Women — the Reserve Army of Army Labour', Cynthia Enloe, *Review of Radical
Political Economics*, Vol. 12 no. 2, Summer 1980.

Periodicals which regularly cover some aspects of the debates
included here

American Friends Service Committee Peacework, AFSC, 2161 Massachusetts
Avenue, Cambridge, Mass 02140, USA.
Catcall, occasional (women only) from 37 Wortley Avenue, London E6.
International Feminism and Nonviolence Newsletter, occasional from Jenny Jacobs,
2 College Close, Buckleigh, Westward Ho!, Devon EX39 1BL.

ISIS, C.P. 50 (Cornavin), 1211 Geneva 2, Switzerland, and Via S. Maria
    dell'Anima 30, Rome, Italy.
Off Our Backs, monthly, from 1841 Columbia Road North West, Room 212,
    Washington DC 20009, USA.
The Pacifist, monthly, from Peace Pledge Union, 6 Endsleigh Street, London WC1.
Peace News, Fortnightly, from 8 Elm Avenue, Nottingham.
Sanity, monthly, from CND, 11 Goodwin Street, London N4.
Spare Rib, monthly, from 27 Clerkenwell Close, London EC1.
War Resisters' International Newsletter, bi-monthly, from WRI, 55 Dawes Street,
    London SE17.
WIN, fortnightly, from 326 Livingstone Street, Brooklyn, NY 11217, USA.
Women's Report (1973-79, bi-monthly). Back issues available from 18 Nibthwaite
    Avenue, Harrow, Middlesex.

Useful Addresses

Campaign Against the Arms Trade, 5 Caledonian Road, London N1 (01 278 1976).
Campaign for Nuclear Disarmament, 11 Goodwin Street, London N4 (01 263 0977).
Commonweal Library, c/o JB Priestley Library, The University, Bradford 7.
Fellowship of Reconciliation, 9 Coombe Road, New Malden, Surrey (01 942 6521).
Feminism and Nonviolence Study Group, c/o 2 College Close, Buckleigh, Westward
    Ho!, Devon EX39 1BL.
Housmans Bookshop, 5 Caledonian Road, London N1 (01 837 4473).
International Fellowship of Reconciliation, Hof van Sonoy 15-17, 1811 LB Alkmaar
    Netherlands.
National Peace Council, 29 Great James Street, London WC1 (01 242 3228).
Northern Ireland Women's Aid, 143a University Street, Belfast 7 (0232 49041).
Peace Pledge Union, 6 Endsleigh Street, London WC1 (01 387 5501)
Rape Crisis Centre (London) 01 837 1600.
Scottish Women's Aid, 11 St. Colme Street, Edinburgh 3 (031 225 8011).
Sisterwrite Bookshop, 190 Upper Street, London N1 (01 226 9782).
War Resisters' International, 55 Dawes Street, London SE17 (01 703 7189).
Welsh Women's Aid, Incentive House, Adam Street, Cardiff (0222 388291).
WIRES, PO Box 162, Sheffield 1 (National newsletter and contacts, women only).
A Woman's Place, 48 William IV Street, London WC2 (01 836 6081).
Women Against Violence Against Women, Central London, c/o A Woman's Place
    (see above). Other local groups via WIRES or local women's centres.
Women for World Disarmament, North Curry, Taunton, Somerset TA3 6HL (0823
    490207).
Women Oppose the Nuclear Threat, c/o Box 600, Peace News, 8 Elm Avenue,
    Nottingham.
Women's Aid Federation (England), 374 Grays Inn Road, London WC1 (01 837
    9316) and 18 Park Row, Leeds (0532 444060).
Women's International League for Peace and Freedom, 29 Great James Street,
    London WC1 (01 242 4817).
Women's Peace Alliance, c/o Box 240, Peace News, 8 Elm Avenue, Nottingham.
Women's Research and Resources Centre, 190 Upper Street, London N1
    (01 359 5773).
World Disarmament Campaign, 238 Camden Road, London NW1 (01 485 1067).

Supplementary Bibliography

Connexions : An International Feminist Quarterly, from 4228 Telegraph Avenue, Oakland, CA 94609, USA.

Women and Peace, ISIS Documentation Packet Number 1, from ISIS Switzerland, P.O. Box 50, CH-1211 Geneva, 2.

Women: A Journal of Liberation, Vol. 8 No.1, (special issue on 'Peace and War'), from 3028 Greenmount Avenue, Balto., Maryland 21218, USA.

Barbara Deming, *Prison Notes,* Grossman, 1966.

Susan Griffin, *Woman and Nature,* Harper & Row, 1978.

Susan Griffin, *Rape: the Power of Consciousness,* Harper & Row, 1979.

Useful Addresses in the USA

Feminist Anti-Nuclear Task Force, P.O.Box 1320, New Haven, CT 06505

War Resisters' League, 339 Lafayette Street, New York, NY 10013

War Resisters' League West, 85 Carl Street, San Francisco, CA 94117

Women's International League for Peace and Freedom, 1213 Race Street, Philadelphia, PA 19107

Women's Network, American Friends' Service Committee, 1515 Cherry Street, Philadelphia, PA 19102

Women's Peace Camp (Seneca Army Depot), c/o Jennifer Tiffany, 323 Cascadilla Street, Ithaca, NY 14850

Women's Peace Camp (Seneca Army Depot), c/o Resist, 38 Union Square, Somerville, MA 02143

Women's Peace Camp (Seattle), c/o R. Lederman, 313 18th Avenue, Seattle, WA 98122

Women's Pentagon Action — New York City, 339 Lafayette Street, New York, NY 10013.

Explanatory Notes

IRA   Irish Republican Army, the armed wing of Sinn Fein, which seeks a united Ireland and freedom from British rule.

National Front   Fascist movement expounding violently racist doctrines, particularly concerned about Black and Asian immigrants in Britain, and also notoriously sexist and homophobic.

Welfare State   In Britain the welfare state, a comprehensive range of social services, was developed gradually during the 20th century. The term is generally understood to mean that range of benefits enshrined in the Beveridge Report, and incorporated into law after the 2nd world war. It is currently under severe attack by the present Conservative government.

National Health Service   One of the gains of the Welfare State, instituted after the Second World War, to provide free health care for all.

Supplementary Benefit   Means-tested social security payment for unemployed and low-paid.

The Cabinet   The inner circle of government Ministers who meet weekly to advise the Prime Minister and make major government decisions.

Emergency Powers Acts   This legislation gives the government power to declare a temporary state of emergency during which many democratic processes are suspended and government bodies and the armed forces are given extra powers. The use of troops to break public sector strikes is only the most visible of these powers.

Luxulyan, Cornwall   When the Central Electricity Generating Board began test-drilling for a possible nuclear reactor site at Luxulyan in the county of Cornwall local people chained themselves to the rig to stop the work, as part of a non-violent protest campaign. Another site was eventually chosen.

Torness   Construction site of Britain's latest nuclear power plant, about 30 miles from Edinburgh. A nonviolent mass occupation took place in May 1979.

Falklands War   On 2 April 1982 Argentinian forces invaded the islands in the South Atlantic known in (and claimed by) Britain as the Falkland Islands and known in (and claimed by) Argentina as Las Malvinas. Britain despatched a 'Task Force' which eventually retook the islands after fighting which lasted until mid June 1982. The islands have 1800 inhabitants. An approximate total of 2500 servicemen and 3 civilian women lost their lives.

Soho 16   Women arrested following a 'Reclaim the Night' march in 1978 in Soho, London's glossy sex shop and red light area.

Seven demands   These seven demands were formulated by the Women's Liberation Movement in Britain between 1970 and 1978.

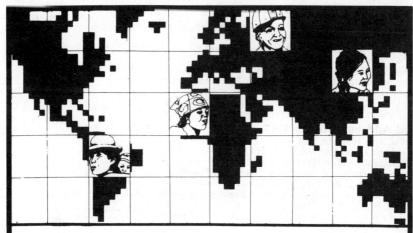